D1310996

BREAK THE GLASS

BREAK
THE GLASS

+ + +

Jean Valentine

Copper Canyon Press

Port Townsend, Washington

Cover art: Antony Gormley, *Another Place*, 1997. Cast iron, 100 elements / 189 × 53 × 29 cm. Installation view, Cuxhaven, Germany. Photograph by Helmut Kunde, Kiel. Copyright Antony Gormley.

Copper Canyon Press is in residence at Fort Worden State Park in Port Townsend, Washington, under the auspices of Centrum. Centrum is a gathering place for artists and creative thinkers from around the world, students of all ages and backgrounds, and audiences seeking extraordinary cultural enrichment.

LIBRARY OF CONGRESS CATALOGING-IN-PUBLICATION DATA
Valentine, Jean.
Break the glass / Jean Valentine.
p. cm.
Includes bibliographical references.
ISBN 978-1-55659-321-5 (alk. paper)
1. Title.
PS3572.A39B74   2010
811'.54—dc22
2010011331

3 5 7 9 8 6 4 2
FIRST PRINTING

Copper Canyon Press
Post Office Box 271
Port Townsend, Washington 98368
www.coppercanyonpress.org

for Kate and Max Greenstreet

ACKNOWLEDGMENTS

Alaska Quarterly Review

The American Poetry Review

Blackbird

Chicago Review

The Cortland Review

Field

Great River Review

The Laurel Review

The Massachusetts Review

Narrative

The Nation

The New Yorker

PMS

Poetry International

upstreet

"Lucy" was published in Sarabande Books'
Quarternote Chapbook Series in 2009.

Heartfelt gratitude to Kaveh Bassiri, Sarah Heller, Joan Larkin,
Jan Heller Levi, Jack Lynch, Anne Marie Macari, and Stephanie Smith;
and to everyone at the MacDowell Colony, Ucross, and at
Sarabande Books and Copper Canyon Press.

a pencil
for a wing-bone
LORINE NIEDECKER

Contents

I

In prison   5

The whitewashed walls   6

The Leopard   7

Even all night long   8

I was working   9

"As with rosy steps the morn"   10

Dear Family,   11

Canoe   12

The Japanese garden   13

Ghost Elephants   14

On a Passenger Ferry   15

Then Abraham   16

Traveler   17

Coyote   18

Hawkins Stable   19

II

Who watches   23

Time is matter here   24

Earth and the Librarian   25

Her car   26

The World inside This One   27

Poet   28

(Two were seen leaving.)   29

The treeless hill   30

The just-born rabbits   31

The valley   32

On the bus   33

The branches   34

Red cloth   35

III

Don't silence yourself, *No te calles*   39

Eurydice who guides   40

If a Person Visits Someone in a Dream, in Some
    Cultures the Dreamer Thanks Them   41

I dropped a plate   43

Desert Prison   44

You ask,   45

The Young Mother   46

I thought It's time   47

On the CD, in the rainstorm   48

Old love, I want to phone you   49

Diana   50

The older man among us   51

He Disappeared into Complete Silence   52

I am fain a page in the court of space   53

IV

Lucy 57

Notes 79
About the Author 81

BREAK THE GLASS

I

+++

In prison

In prison
without being accused

or reach your family
or have a family   You have

conscience
heart trouble

asthma
manic-depressive

(we lost the baby)
no meds

no one
no window

black water
nail-scratched walls

your pure face turned away
embarrassed

you
who the earth was for.

The whitewashed walls

The whitewashed walls, the chair
Were we nursed by the same wet-nurse?

The cups of tea undrunk
The crumb of tobacco on your lip

The poems in our speckled notebooks
where we warmed our hands

over the quick fire

Long before the woodstove's wood and coal
shifted and settled and warmed us

Even months before
Even from miles away

The Leopard

Like a leopard on a shield, the space leopard
lay down beside the basket,
and slowly I threw all the papers in.
I was glad to throw them in.

Every coldness ever breathed
had left its trace elements inside me;
the oldest mother god's most silent love
had left its trace: her
cave paintings black and gold
& red in the caves of my body.

In the end,
I laid them all down there at the leopard's feet,
I was glad to lay them down.

Even all night long

Even all night long while
the night train

pulls me on in my dream
like a needle

Even then, down in my bed
my hand across the sheet

anyone's hand
my face anyone's face

are held
and kissed

the water
the child

the friend
unlost.

I was working

I was working on cleaning up a house
before I left it.

The longest work every year was Clean the house
before we moved.

The mother as a child was always moving,
who knows why.

I, said the fly.
With my little eye.

If I clean up this house here long enough,
I can leave it.

But leave the eye next to where I
put my house, this way, that way—

"As with rosy steps the morn"

in memory of Lorraine Hunt Lieberson

Everyone
on the other side of the earth
standing upside down, listening,
Everyone on the reverse of the picture
on the other side of the measuring eye

The five notes, slowly, over & over,
and with some light intent,
And the whole air,
no edge, no center,

And the light so thin, so fast—

+

Don't listen to the words—
they're only little shapes for what you're saying,
they're only cups if you're thirsty, you aren't thirsty.

Dear Family,

> "[the chrysalises] came out with their wings
> packed down... like crumpled letters... Some
> did not get quite free... "
>
> REBECCA SOLNIT, *A Field Guide to Getting Lost*

November 1862. Dear Family,

Lying here tonight, looking into the fire, waiting for fire,
I was seeing our fire at home, in my mind's eye:
Mother, the little girls—
but then gunfire— we took up our guns
I'd have gone forward, but
then went the right eye of my body,

                        Mother,
don't read this yet,
my thoughts are still packed down
like crumpled letters, and some of us
will not get quite free—

Canoe

Listen to the crescent
Listen to
the thin old house

Black Elk
smoking with us

pulling to us
up to the late dock
the canoe

Not enough bark
It was stretched till it broke
Patched, pale colors

An old horse, almost completely blind

A map
to *the end of this world or cycle*

The Japanese garden

The Japanese garden
is tilting quietly uphill

—eleven wet green stones,
bamboo, and ferns—

It might be under water,
the birds be fish, colored in.   And you,

masked reader: the glance
of your underwater lamp,

your blackwater embrace—
not bought or sold.

Ghost Elephants

In the elephant field
tall green ghost elephants
with your cargo of summer leaves

at night I heard you breathing at the window

Don't you ever think I'm not crying
since you're away from me
Don't ever think I went free

At first the goodbye had a lilt to it—
maybe just a couple of months—
but it was a beheading.

Ghost elephant,
reach down,
cross me over—

On a Passenger Ferry

in memory of Grace Paley

The deck is big, and crowded. In one corner,
an old woman, sick, on chemo, not in pain, is
writing in an elementary school notebook.
Nobody else saw her, but I saw her.
I had seen her before. Her round, kind face,
smiling and still as a photograph
outside a window—

Then Abraham

Then an old man came down out of the thicket,
with an axe on his shoulder, and with him

two people made out of light
—one a blameless son,

the other like a Vermeer girl,
on their way back down with the old man.

Still, all the history of the world
happens at once: In the rain, a young man

holds out a blue cloth
to caress her head

at the landing-pier
of the new bride.

You can't get beauty. (Still,
in its longing it flies to you.)

Traveler

A matchbox painted and figured
with five gardeners
and thirty-seven flowers, red and blue,
a pretty garden.
One little fellow stands off.
Anybody can see
love is all around him,
like the blue air. Most
dear in the Double Realm
of music, he is a Traveler.
He stands off, alone.
When somebody dies, as is the custom,
he burns the place down.

Coyote

Walking last night in the drought-country dark
she heard wolves howl. No,
coyotes.

Sexual love
coyotes crying
breathing close

This morning it was on the radio
it's turning a little cooler, she is turning

She has given her purse of money
away, it's time
to turn back into Coyote

My, my Coyote in the doorway

Hawkins Stable

It was years before you could climb
back up over the fallen stalls, and knock at
the family's old door

                    —they were gone,
you could just look in from the road.
Field after field.
Your eyes looked two ways at once.

                              Under the fields,
the dense tongue of the cow—
and the horses' eyes—

and the water from the hand-pump in the sink,
racing like horses.

II

+ + +

Who watches

for Dr. Paul Farmer

Who watches
on a moon-surface hillside
the soon-dead children's rubber ball
circle in an oval
sunstruck orbit,
from hand to hand...
Cange,
Haiti,
Earth

Time is matter here

Time *is* matter here
The freight train
I saw in the morning
still in the evening
inching across the flatlands
word after slow word
too many to count

And you are matter—
your eyes, your long legs,
slow breath sometimes catching
in your sleep, your head
resting against the bus window,
tired horse,
tired rider

Earth and the Librarian

At the library
she passed a tray with little
books of baked earth on it—

—*Take one,*
and eat it;
It is sweet,
and it is given for you.

—*Who lives in me?*
said Earth—

Her car

Her car had hit another car.
The other driver's insurance person called.

It was all going well,
a matter of time.

She lost her tongue. It was her taste
for life, for herself, for others.

She found her tongue on the floor
and paper-clipped it to

the kitchen calendar. This was back in the day
of Separation. Permanence.

The World inside This One

There is another world
but it is inside this one
ÉLUARD

Steamer trunks
standing on end
standing open
like big books

The world inside of that one
mass graves
like in this one

Inside of that world
someone painting
animal-souls

Inside the dark
huge sounds

Poet

I'm standing there
behind your grandparents, proud,
saying goodbye:

you with your three dresses,
your prettiness,
going up to the city—and beside you
the devoted, tall shadowy monk.
(Two were seen leaving.)

(Two were seen leaving.)

And inside them   deep space
And deepspace loves them

moving slowly its thumb
across to the speck of gold there
there on her lip

but not hunger

or hunger not granted

The treeless hill

The treeless hill that gave holes
in its dirt cliff to the swallows
in the long wet light of June, the open
cliff by the road that gave
them nests, your cold wet sweater,
sweater you were born in, softer then,
like any swallow

The just-born rabbits

The just-born rabbits in the garden
huddled blind, translucent, hardly here

I called John (a farmer),
and asked him what to do:

Put your boot on them. Now you've been there,
the mother will never come back.

—life from whom
death also springeth green
—thy leave to sleep

The valley

The valley
edge by edge
bare field by field
I walked through it through you

rain by rain
cold by cold
root absence
and the purposeful cold

Eye opened
slow
but what is slow

On the bus

the ghost-bus travels along beside us
and the reading-light,
a straight-faced little moon

And you cloud, ragged, legless rabbit
with your long nose
and your enormous eye

Tell me
What is the name for a non-endstopped line?
Who was it M. looked like?

Was it Kafka?   Kafka,
is that your enormous eye?
Ecstatic eye,
still see us   your same clay

The branches

The branches looked first like tepees,
but there was no emptiness.

Like piles of leaves waiting for fire:
at the foot of the wisewoman trees,
at the foot of the broken General.

Next to the tree of the veteran
girl who died this summer   slow red
cloth

Red cloth

Red cloth
I lie on the ground
otherwise nothing could hold

I put my hand on the ground
the membrane is gone
and nothing does hold

your place in the ground
is all of it
and it is breathing

III

+++

Don't silence yourself, No te calles

He took some words from the bowl
and placed them on the table
No te calles

I took some too
placed them near to his words
     Martín Ramírez

After,   slowly, slowly
from childhood
towards him   followed my footsteps

circling sometimes
sometimes falling   in a quite practical way
to sleep   to speak

Eurydice who guides

Eurydice who guides   Orpheus who guides
who first has to return to death
the one who sings
the one who opens first
of all the animals his
mouth to her song
her thirst his thirst
the ones who nurse each other

Don't be afraid the blackened saucepan said
I met them in the country by a well
and once I drank from them
I never thirst

If a Person Visits Someone in a Dream, in Some Cultures the Dreamer Thanks Them

in memory of Reginald Shepherd

Dear Reginald,
It is morning.
I sit at a table
writing a letter
with a needle and thread.

✦

I pricked my finger   A pelican
out of her migratory path,
even her language family—
whose child is gone
yet she absently pecks at her breast.

✦

I write on the bedspread
I am making for you there
May you breathe deeply and easily.
If a person visits someone in a dream,
in some cultures the dreamer thanks them in the morning
for visiting their dream.

✦

I call it dream
not that I am drawn to that which withdraws
but to him *pearled, asleep,* who never withdraws.

+

At a hotel in another star. The rooms were cold and
damp, we were both at the desk at midnight asking if
they had any heaters. They had one heater. You are
ill, please you take it. Thank you for visiting my dream.

+

Can you breathe all right?
Break the glass   shout
break the glass   force the room
break the thread   Open
the music behind the glass.

+

Remember that blue vine?   Grown
                alongside the gate

fourteenth century
                Venus close as the moon

the bowl of the skull   turning here
                        lifting that

I dropped a plate

I dropped a plate and broke it
it came from a set

I keep the scraped-down leak marks from the rain
on the wall from two years ago
layers blue and tan

Page 7

Page 8

The broken, the underneath,
the backwards:

On the radio, Merce said, *Do it backwards,*
Jump first, then run,
even if it was just with his arms, when he got old,
even if some people hated it

Desert Prison

If every present is possible,
how can we have eyes to see?

The teacher and I, the guest, both free, class over,
just walking down the corridor, out to the gate

The teacher and I, looking wildly
how to mend
the man's head that the other man had stabbed—

Where to wash
your head   that they had stabbed

You kneeling, by the door,
trying to get out of the corridor—

You ask,

Could we have coffee?   —No, my truth,
I'm still on this side.
        I saw you last night, again,

at the bar on 57th,
O faceless dancer,
and I put down my mask

I wanted you to touch me
You stood there neither man nor woman,
beautiful edge   by the water

The Young Mother

Milk called out of the breast
to the just-born mouth

Inside the earth
earth came

All membrane
no sound

—orgasm—god—
be my unshareable secret?   unreceived?

I'm sad, Warden
Are you sad

All you people looking out from the stern
of the white ship *Withholding*

—I'll take my babies
and swim

I thought It's time

I thought It's time to go into the forest with a bowl.

Maya said, *It's all one thing,*
student, householder, forest.

The blue man said,
You are the forest and the bowl

—as he made a trail of tobacco, or cornmeal,
back to the foot of my chair.

Jack said,
You don't need
a bowl. Putting his cupped hands together
in front of him on Eighth Street

—the trees walking toward us
hands cupped in the light of Eighth Street.

On the CD, in the rainstorm

in memory of Michal Kunz

On the CD, in the rainstorm
the healer whispers what he hears from his guides.
His whispers are a quiet-stepping rainstorm
stepping across the room.

                    Michal
—I hope you don't mind my saying this—
sits down with us and looks up into the rain.
They say
he will write
if not his poems
other poems.

Old love, I want to phone you

I miss another body in this life.   But miss
you, turned-away?
Can I miss not-love? The centuries say
Sure possible, all the languages say, all the
bodies, the trees. Ice storms.
                    In her room
a student cuts angular lines
into her arm.
The blue man says, *Don't cut, they're saying* (he listens, whispers,
then he talks) *they're saying   For the present
A body by herself cán be in love on earth.*

Diana

The tab on the tea bag said
"Love what is ahead
by loving what has come before."
But what came before was no dream
you wake from, it was human sacrifice:
Diana was herself, and Actaeon, who saw her naked,
and the stag he was turned into
(who was God)
and the blind dogs
and the death of God
"for the sin of seeing."   God
still childbearing, naked, seeing.
Do we get another life?   *Oh yes.*
Maybe not in this place.   Maybe in different forms.

So, what do you think?

Book Title: _____

Comments: _____
_____
_____
_____

Can we quote you on that? ☐ yes ☐ no

Copper Canyon Press seeks to build the awareness of, appreciation of, and audience for a wide range of emerging and established American poets, as well as poetry in translation from many of the world's cultures, classical and contemporary. To receive our catalog, send us this postage-paid card or email your contact information to poetry@coppercanyonpress.org

NAME: _____

ADDRESS: _____

CITY: _____

STATE: _____ ZIP: _____

EMAIL: _____

☐ Send me *Editor's Choice*, a bimonthly email of poems from forthcoming titles.

COPPER CANYON PRESS

www.coppercanyonpress.org

The older man among us

The older man among us looked right through me.   Lost.
Without expression.   Long look.   Who were you?
I had a glass of water in my hand.
Are you my grandfather?   Would you like to drink?
I wished I was a horse, and I could lay
my head over your neck.

He Disappeared into Complete Silence

The wild ladders of longing
no longer pieces of wild wood, sawed off
and fitted to each other,
no longer stored in a closed-off room
with one blank window

But called back, through
the closed-off wooden ceiling, to his
speech returned.

I am fain a page in the court of space

I have pulled the elements in no order
in around me, like a blanket:
elephant blanket.
It will harden when I take it off,
my skin, when I
leave you on the ground and walk away.

A page   air
a pen   water
books   earth
friends   fire

IV

+++

Lucy

for Sister Leslie, C.H.S.

Lucy, whose skeleton is approximately 3.2 million years old, whose genus and species are *"Australopithecus afarensis*, or 'southern ape of Afar,' after the region of Ethiopia where the bones were found," was discovered in 1974, at Hadar in northern Ethiopia. "The Ethiopian people refer to her as 'Dinkenesh,' an Amharic language term meaning 'You are beautiful.'"

Lucy
your secret book
that you leaned over and wrote just in the dirt—
Not having to have an ending
Not having to last

...in thy book all my members
were written, which in continuance
were fashioned, when as yet there
was none of them.

PSALM 139:16

Two hands
were all you owned

for food
for love

Now you own none, Lucy
nor no words

only
breath marks

breath marks
only

nor no words
Or what *do* you do now Lucy

for love?
Your eyeholes.

Lucy
my saxifrage that splits the rocks
wildgood
mother
you fill my center-hole
with bliss
No one is so tender in her scream
Wants me so much
Not just, but brings me to be   Is
when I am close to death
and close to life

The spider
in her web three days
dead on the window Lucy

In the electricity of love, its lightning strike
or in its quiet hum in the thighs
like this little icebox here
not knowing any better
or in the dumb hum of the heater going on
little stirs in the room-tone
I rush outdoors into the air you are
Lucy
and you rush out to receive me
At last there you are
who I always *knew* was there
but almost died not
meeting
        when my scraped-out child died Lucy
you hold her, all the time.

Lucy
when the dark bodies
dropped out of the towers

When Ruth died
and Grace
and Helen Ruth

And Iraq
and Iraq

And Nikolay

Lucy, when Jane in her last clothes
goes across   with Chekhov
you are the ferryman, the monk
Ieronim
who throws your weight on the rope.

I wash my plate and spoon
as carefully as a priest.
Did you have a cup, Lucy?
O God who transcends time,
let Lucy have a cup.
You bodhisattva here-
with-us. You wanted to come back!
I'm afraid
and can't pay attention
to it   I'm
wild with heat and cold
and my head hurts:
The nine wild turkeys come up calmly to the porch
to see you, Lucy

My Work of Art

for Lucy

It's a piece of brown wrapping paper
taped to the wall   over the table
in this beautiful room with no pictures
First, written across the top:
"It was as if she was standing
across the road
waiting to see if anyone
wanted to get to know her."

Then taped under that:

Du, der du weißt, und dessen weites Wissen

> *You who know, and whose vast knowing*
> *is born of poverty, abundance of poverty—*

> *make it so the poor are no longer*
> *despised and thrown away.*

Look at them standing about
like wildflowers, which have nowhere else to grow.

Then a blue panther, a twenty-six-cent stamp
from Florida, for postcards

Then a catalpa leaf curving
from its huge curving stem, the leaf

a little broken in its passing
from the West down to the East

and the note: I found this leaf
on my way to the Post Office.

Then Lucy you: hominid? sapiens?
sapere, to taste, be wise

Your skeleton
standing about, like a wildflower...

Lucy, what you want,
that I will do.
To hear you now.
Your poem. (But you need nothing.)

The deer and the wild turkeys
that draw close now to hear you.
My life is for.
In its language.
Your voice.

I can't tell cold from heat.
Anxiety
dust.
Death, no
not even dust.

Your Picture

Brown museum hair, brushed the way they brush it there,
brow lit from inside,
intelligent eyebrows,
a slightly wrinkly nose, a little flat—
brown woman, I want your nose, your
cheekbones of light—I was brown, I got white—
Your large and friendly mouth, half-open
in a half-smile,
like the Dalai Lama once, in a procession,
his smile "What am I doing here?"

But Lucy
your eyes.

So I gave all I had to the poor, standing about
like wildflowers.

Lucy,
the spider moved, last night,
and again, this morning...

I wonder Do you sleep and wake
where you are now? Do spiders
hibernate? Do they lay eggs
in webs on windowpanes?

                        You must know
everything.

Enter the sweet Why
Don't entreat it
or question why
whistle why
whisper why
was sweetness done to you
done unto you
What I wanted most   the mother
has come to me
Will she stay in my ear? Lucy
Is it you?
Still all night long my
Lucy I entreat you
I will not let thee go except thou bless me.

Outsider Art

Martín Ramírez,
be with me!
"It looks just like a vagina,"
a bystander said. Yes
it is a vagina, with trains, and tunnels,
and like in the great cathedrals,
a clitoris, a starry one,
and a womb, jaunty Martín being born, Lucy
did you hear animal-woman
screams in the night?
Were you afraid?
Was it you last night
your scream over and over
as you give birth?

How did you pray, Lucy?
You *were* prayer.
Your hands and toes.
When writing came back to me
I prayed with lipstick
on the windshield
as I drove.
Newton made up with the world,
he had already turned himself
into gold, he was already there.

Skeleton Woman,
in   down
over   around

Bless:
from the Old English *blētsian.*
Its root is *blood.*

My head is at your window, Lucy, at your glass,

But we offer nothing but money now,
we beam it to each other near and far,

But you are my skeleton mother,
I bring you
coffee in your cemetery bed.

This morning I miss most of all you, Martín,
and her who when you were born
looked and blessed your beauty.
Lucy, when you are with me
I feel the atoms
racing everywhere
in this old oak table,
in the eight-pointed double-star spider,
and in the starry rippling all around us.

Skeleton Woman, Guardian, Death Woman, Lucy,
Here, a picnic, corn bread, here, an orange
with Martín and me at the lip of the Earth Surface World.

Notes

"The branches" is for Jody Gladding.

"Diana": the poem draws on Norman O. Brown's "Metamorphoses II: Actaeon."

"He Disappeared into Complete Silence": Louise Bourgeois, plate 8, 1947.

LUCY

62   The Holy Bible, King James Version.

64   "my saxifrage that splits the rocks"—see "A Sort of a Song," by William Carlos Williams: "Saxifrage is my flower that splits / the rocks." *The William Carlos Williams Reader,* New Directions, 1966.

66   Nikolay and Ieronim are in Chekhov's story "Easter Eve," in *The Bishop and Other Stories,* translated by Constance Garnett, The Ecco Press, 1985.

68–69 Rainer Maria Rilke, *Rilke's Book of Hours,* translated by Anita Barrows and Joanna Macy, Riverhead Trade, 2005.

74   Martín Ramírez was a Mexican immigrant painter who lived for fifteen years in DeWitt State Hospital in California, until his death in 1963. His work was shown at the American Folk Art Museum in New York City in 2007.

About the Author

Jean Valentine was born in Chicago, earned her B.A. from Radcliffe College, and has lived most of her life in New York City. She won the Yale Younger Poets Award for her first book, *Dream Barker*, in 1965. Her collection *Door in the Mountain: New and Collected Poems, 1965–2003*, was the winner of the 2004 National Book Award for Poetry. Her work has also received a Guggenheim Fellowship and awards from the NEA, the Bunting Institute (now the Radcliffe Institute), the Rockefeller Foundation, the New York State Council on the Arts, and the New York Foundation for the Arts, as well as the Maurice English Award, the Teasdale Poetry Prize, the Poetry Society of America's Shelley Memorial Award, the Morton Dauwen Zabel Award from the American Academy of Arts and Letters, the Wallace Stevens Award from the Academy of American Poets, and a fellowship from Lannan Foundation.

Lannan Literary Selections

For two decades Lannan Foundation has supported the
publication and distribution of exceptional literary works.
Copper Canyon Press gratefully acknowledges their support.

LANNAN LITERARY SELECTIONS 2010

Stephen Dobyns, *Winter's Journey*

Travis Nichols, *See Me Improving*

James Richardson, *By the Numbers*

John Taggart, *Is Music: Selected Poems*

Jean Valentine, *Break the Glass*

RECENT LANNAN LITERARY SELECTIONS
FROM COPPER CANYON PRESS

Michael Dickman, *The End of the West*

James Galvin, *As Is*

David Huerta, *Before Saying Any of the Great Words: Selected Poems,*
translated by Mark Schafer

Sarah Lindsay, *Twigs and Knucklebones*

Heather McHugh, *Upgraded to Serious*

W.S. Merwin, *Migration: New & Selected Poems*

Valzhyna Mort, *Factory of Tears,* translated by Franz Wright
and Elizabeth Oehlkers Wright

Taha Muhammad Ali, *So What: New & Selected Poems, 1971–2005,*
translated by Peter Cole, Yahya Hijazi, and Gabriel Levin

Lucia Perillo, *Inseminating the Elephant*

Ruth Stone, *In the Next Galaxy*

Connie Wanek, *On Speaking Terms*

C.D. Wright, *One Big Self: An Investigation*

For a complete list of Lannan Literary Selections from
Copper Canyon Press, please visit Partners on our Web site:
www.coppercanyonpress.org

The Chinese character for poetry is made up of two parts: "word" and "temple." It also serves as pressmark for Copper Canyon Press.

Since 1972, Copper Canyon Press has fostered the work of emerging, established, and world-renowned poets for an expanding audience. The Press thrives with the generous patronage of readers, writers, booksellers, librarians, teachers, students, and funders — everyone who shares the belief that poetry is vital to language and living.

Major funding has been provided by:

Amazon.com

Anonymous

Beroz Ferrell & The Point, LLC

Golden Lasso, LLC

Lannan Foundation

National Endowment for the Arts

Cynthia Lovelace Sears and Frank Buxton

William and Ruth True

Washington State Arts Commission

Charles and Barbara Wright

For information and catalogs:

COPPER CANYON PRESS
Post Office Box 271
Port Townsend, Washington 98368
360-385-4925
www.coppercanyonpress.org

Copper Canyon Press gratefully acknowledges board member Jim Wickwire in honor of his many years of service to poetry and independent publishing.

The typeface is Janson Text, created by Hungarian traveling scholar Nicholas Kis in the 1680s. Adrian Frutiger and others at Linotype contributed to this 1985 digital version. Book design and composition by Valerie Brewster, Scribe Typography. Printed on archival-quality paper at McNaughton & Gunn, Inc.